Have I given you my CONSENT?

Kim May

Illustrated by Anisha Singha

Text and illustration copyright © Kim May 2020

ISBN: 978-0-6484740-2-9

All rights reserved. No part of this book may be reproduced, stored in or introduced into a retrieval system, or transmitted, in any form or by means (electronic, mechanical, photocopying, recording or otherwise) without written permission of the copyright owner Kim May.

Typesetting and layout: WorkingType www.workingtype.com.au

Published July 2020

This book is dedicated to all children learning their right to give or not give consent.

I may not say how I feel

When someone tickles my body and makes me squeal

But one thing I know that needs to be said

Is have I given them my CONSENT?

I may not say "I don't like that"

When someone lifts me on to their lap

But one thing I know that needs to be said

Is have I given them my CONSENT?

I may not say that I want to flee
When someone's hands are touching me
But one thing I know that needs to be said
Is have I given them my CONSENT?

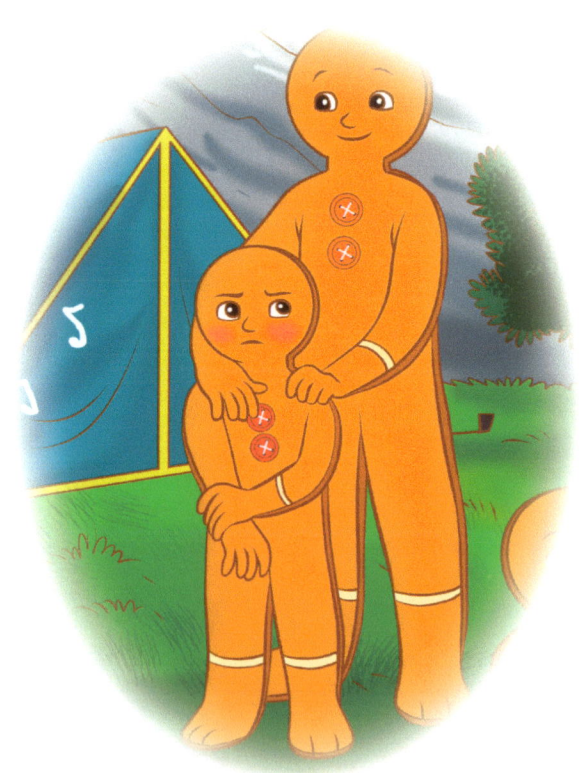

I may not say that I like my space

When someone gives me a big embrace

But one thing I know that needs to be said

Is have I given them my CONSENT?

I may not say "I don't like to be kissed"

Even when it's someone that I have missed

But one thing I know that needs to be said

Is have I given them my CONSENT?

I may not say "I don't want you to see"

When I'm in the bathroom having a wee

But one thing I know that needs to be said

Is have I given you my CONSENT?

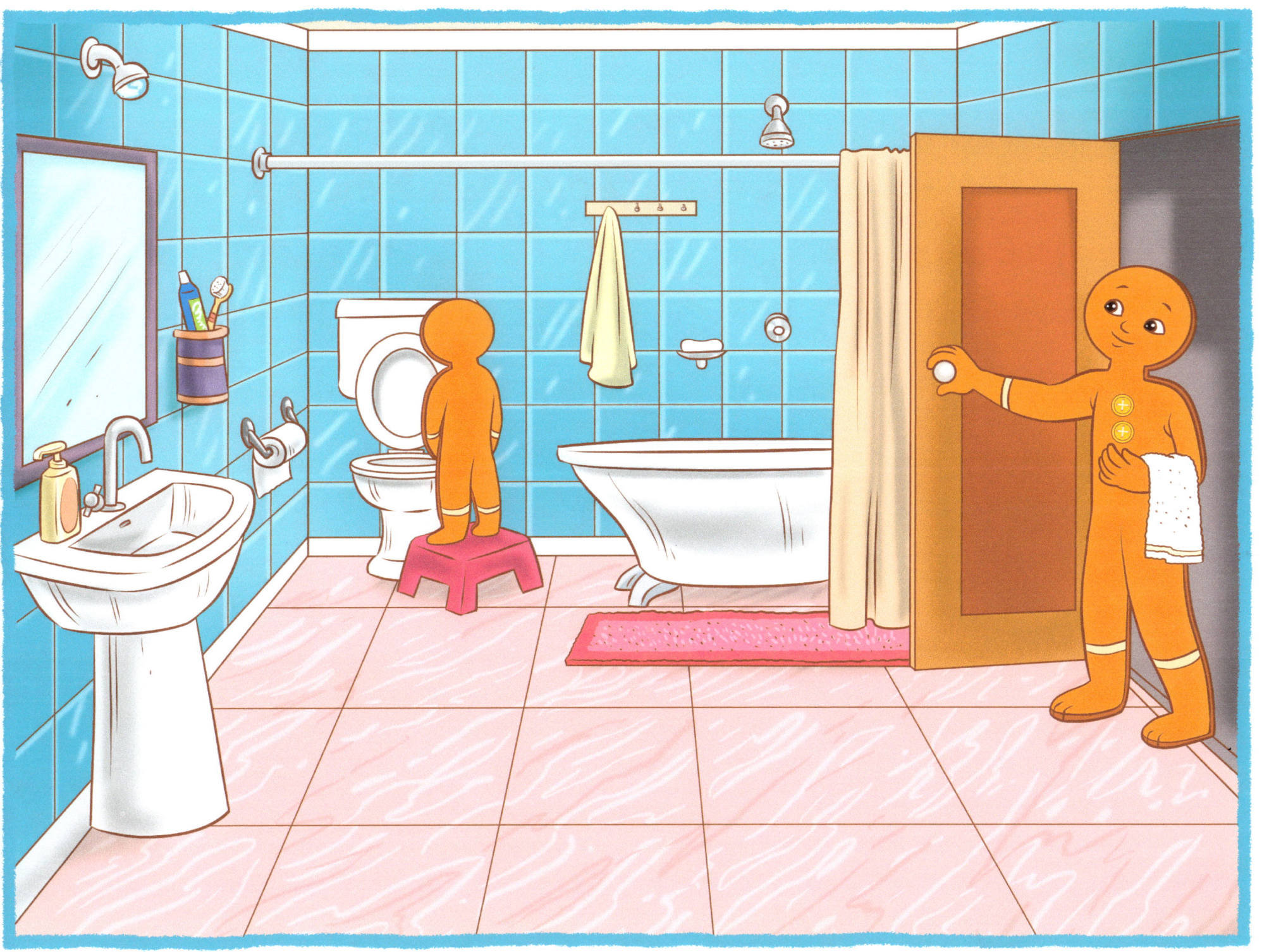

I may not say not to come in

When I am getting ready to wash my skin

But one thing I know that needs to be said

Is have I given you my CONSENT?

I may not say that it feels rotten

When someone strange wipes my bottom

But one thing I know that needs to be said

Is have I given them my CONSENT?

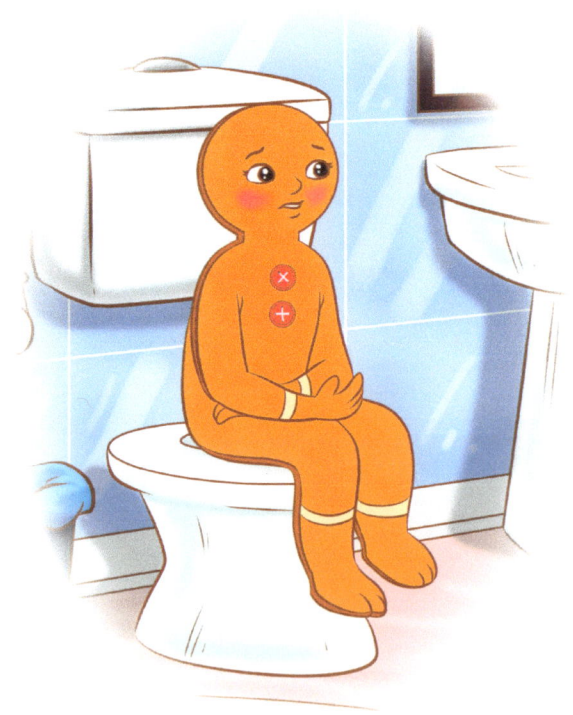

I may not say that I feel stressed

When someone enters and I am not dressed

But one thing I know that needs to be said

Is have I given them my CONSENT?

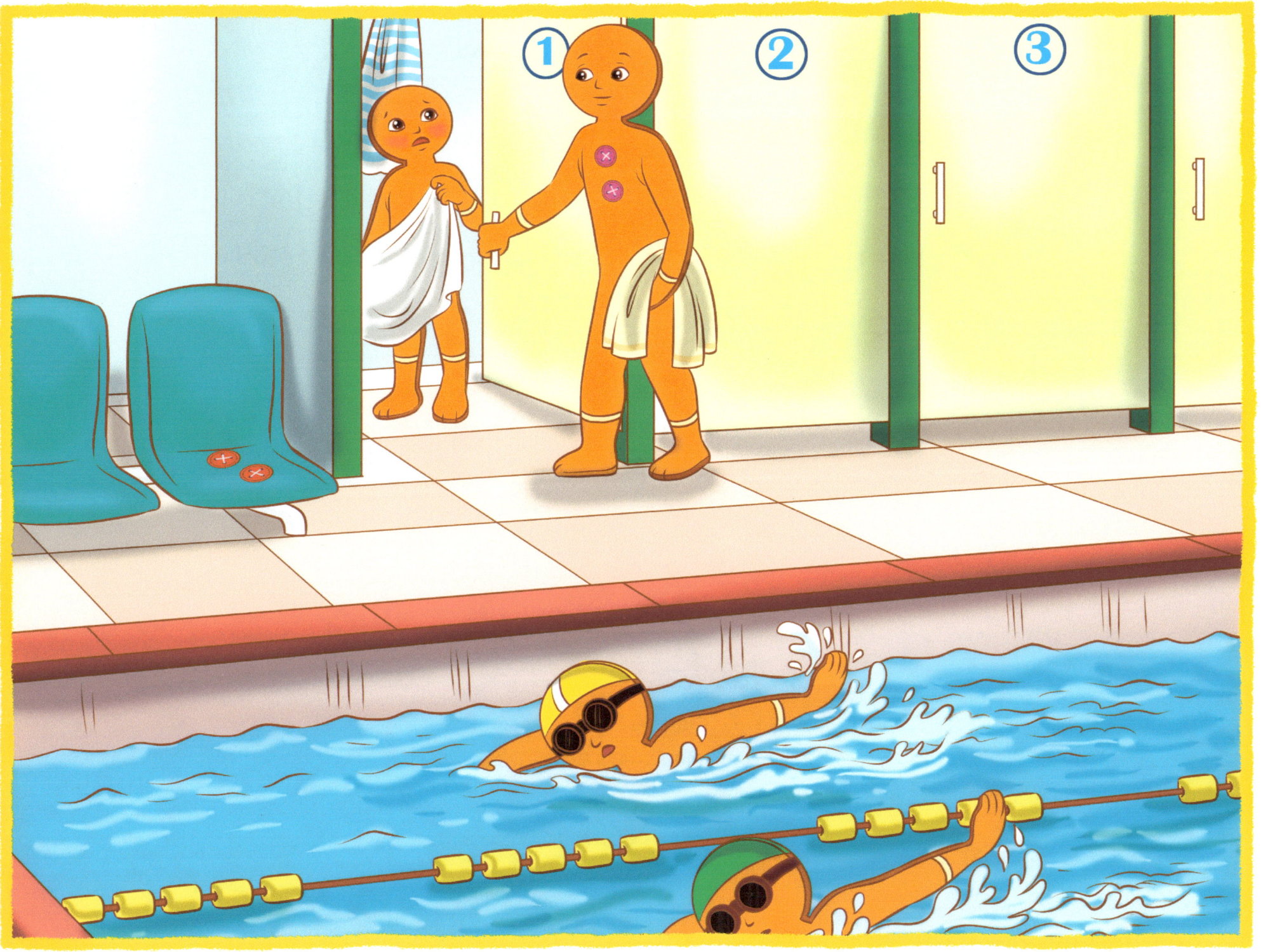

I may not say that I get a fright

When someone enters my room at night

But one thing I know that needs to be said

Is have I given them my CONSENT?

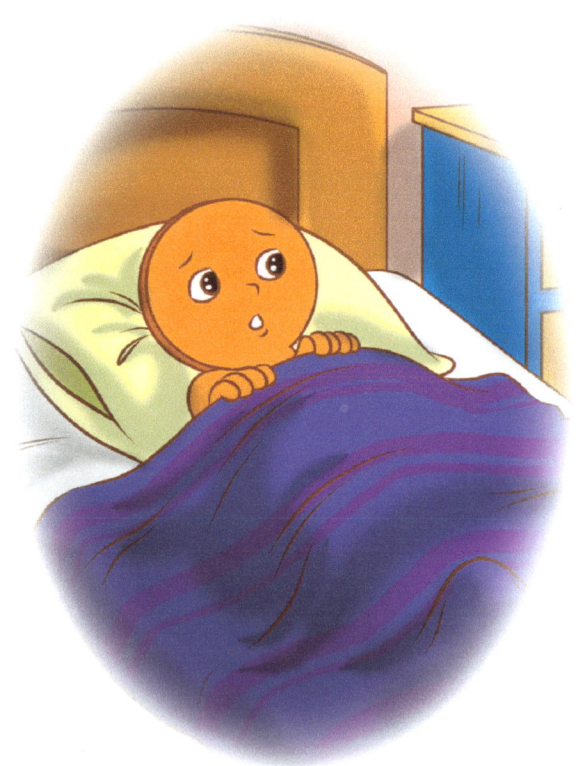

I may not say that I don't like

People taking my photo to put online

But one thing I know that needs to be said

Is have I given them my CONSENT?

I may not say that I don't feel fine

When someone strange talks to me online

But one thing I know that needs to be said

Is have you, and have I, given them CONSENT?

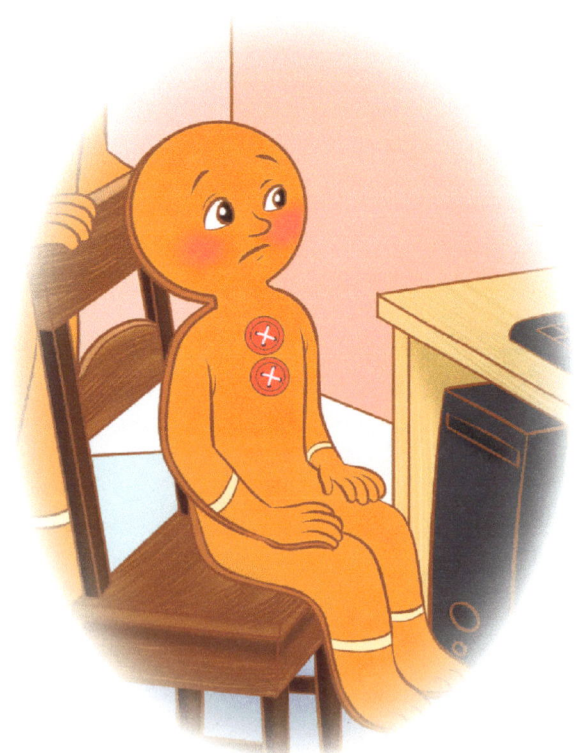

I may not say that I don't want to go

To unfamiliar places that I do not know

But one thing I know that needs to be said

Is have you explained and discussed my CONSENT?

I may not always remember to say

When I am uncomfortable in any way

But from this book I hope you have learnt

That it is my right to make sure that I'm heard

So now that we are clear about what I have said

Be sure that you ask me if I give my CONSENT.

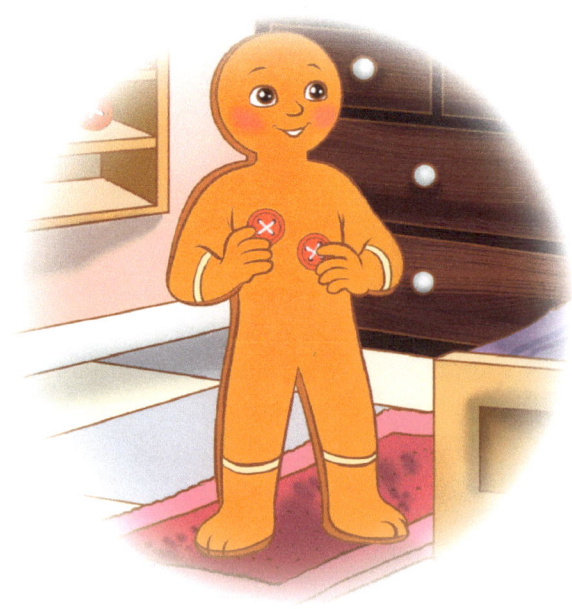

www.ingramcontent.com/pod-product-compliance
Lightning Source LLC
Chambersburg PA
CBHW050853010526

44107CB00047BA/1598